THE JUPITER C

The Jupiter Collisions

LACHLAN MACKINNON

ff

faber and faber

First published in 2003
by Faber and Faber Ltd
3 Queen Square London WC1N 3AU
Published in the United States by Faber and Faber Inc.,
an affiliate of Farrar, Straus and Giroux LLC, New York

Typeset by Wilmaset Ltd, Birkenhead, Wirral
Printed in Great Britain by
TJ International Ltd, Padstow, Cornwall
All rights reserved

A CIP record for this book
is available from the British Library

ISBN 0-571-21655-2

2 4 6 8 10 9 7 5 3 1

To W.
with love

Acknowledgements

Some of these poems first appeared in the *Independent*, the *London Review of Books*, *London Quarterly* and the *Times Literary Supplement*.

'Eve' was commissioned by Dr Trevor Weston, as part of a series of poems linked to paintings by Peter Rodulfo.

Others previously appeared, sometimes in other versions or with other titles, as follows: 'Youth' in *The Poet's View*, ed. Gladys Mary Coles (it is based on Paul Nash's *Landscape of the Moon's Last Phase*); 'Bob Dylan's Minnesota Harmonica Sound' in *Jewels and Binoculars*, ed. Phil Bowen; 'On the Roof of the World' in *Things We Said Today*, ed. Phil Bowen; 'Staying with Friends' and 'For Caroline Fraser' in *New Writing 7*, ed. Carmen Callil and Craig Raine.

Contents

The Jupiter Collisions

Curled like the scrolled end of a chair's arm, swaddled
in dust or gas, the comet's rock or ice heart
    went to bits in the field
of invisible stress round Jupiter;

that was the first pass. At the next, like wagons
of a goods train or boys in Indian file,
    each fragment bowed its head
and fell into the giant's vast embrace.

Artists alone could guess for us what happened,
how a million tongues of fire came falling
    out of the blazing sky
above the unliveable, livid land,

mutely, like semaphore. Nothing could touch us
from those forty-five light-minutes off. Lenses
    noted the high scars. Each
pockmark could have swallowed the earth entire.

Almost dusk, in a hot unyielding summer:
we walked beside the river. Moorhens, homing,
    jerked along as though tugged
by invisible wires, the reeds conferred

in a rustle little louder than a breath,
a bat played at sliding on air and the dark
    water spun lazily
above the weir, holding a withered leaf

in orbit then dashing it to destruction
as would have happened had we not been there. Flakes
    of ammonia snow
as before out of Jupiter's black sky.

Riders on the Storm

for Anna, in Prague

In your quite unimaginably different life,
death grins and beats his little drum each hour.
History, you might say, persuaded you
to abandon history for a life.
On the island, is there still beer in plastic mugs?
The trams run all night, their opening and closing doors
the city's gills. Can we stay young forever?

When we got to Helena's flat, she was just sitting there
writing postcards to absences, her lovely blonde hair
tied with turquoise laces into Hansel-and-Gretel bunches.
What there was in the fridge defied two languages
and in the sleepy ochre courtyard a rusty
metal frame rusted beyond recognition.
Nobody in the world knew where I was

the night before, the one in the building-workers' hostel
(as I learnt later), on a bare-mattressed bed
in an empty double room with a concrete floor, all thanks
to the hard-currency deal I'd struck in the dark.
I pushed everything, passport, money, tickets,
under the pillow and entered a deep sleep
from which I supposed I might never come round.

Nothing was in my hands. So when we got there,
to that oak-panelled flat with its shelves of books
translated from the major tongues, she sat there
like a genius loci, writing messages to loved ones

I envied but would never see. It was like looking upstream into a hinterland of dark woods and lost villages, berries, a swimming-hole, alien, unintelligible jokes.

Water

The upholsterer stood up with a grin
and said, 'Look, money!', offering
what he'd found in the chair's insides, deeper
than you could reach.
                               It's more than ten years
since my father died; those roughly sixty pence
will have trickled out of his pocket as
so often.
            You felt it was like a whisper
carried over a lake, but one so wide
that the other shore was invisible.

As near Ann Arbor, where the great lake slopped
and seemed to stretch forever.
                                I was seven
and I remember nothing of that day,
neither his face nor yours nor any words,
only the endlessness.
                    Flotsam and jetsam,
I'd like to add, but there is only water,
cold grey unlovely water heaped
and furrowed.
            And the cold wind blowing
puckers the nylon of my olive windcheater

in the early sixties.
                    Nothing holds things
together but remembering.
                        They say
the good God will remember everything;

[5]

I hope so.
            Even my whimpering secrets,
if that's what it costs to stand again by grey
musclebound water, vast and meaningless,
which otherwise had meant oblivion.
Gulls rise and shout
                    but not in protest
against the way the world might prove to be.

Staying with Friends

The lawn of marital unhappiness,
the big house and the ha-ha,

the scary stabled horse
I knew could kill me with a kick,

would have been grist
to any gossip columnist,

given the fame
that lapped them all,

but we were children,
lost among the bewildering

tall grasses, quarrels, poppies
and adult silences.

From the South Deeside Road

The little green fishing-hut
where my grandmother used to sit
while her sister and father took fish after fish
is still there.

It is over seventy years,
somebody keeps it up. The same unchanging
endlessly changing water runs.

At Maryculter

A stone cross on a double plinth gazes
across the valley. That white gable end
in a mist of stripped trees is the rented house
where my grandmother's childhood was so happy.

Bearing her ashes like an offering,
the minister climbs the track from the new manse.
His blue clerical shirt echoes the blue sky
of this freakishly bright December day.

The grave is open for the last time,
the family together. She has come home
or gone home. Let the winds blow on Maryculter,
let the snow snow on Maryculter:

when the memorials behind this granite
church of the Church of Scotland are long obscured
by the passage of many winters, I imagine some
passer-by stooping to wipe the moss off her name,

knowing nothing of all this, wondering.

NOTE: Maryculter is pronounced Marycooter.

Youth

Trees mass like sheep,
heads together, conferring.
They are white-fringed like Alps by the backwash
of the light that's beyond them. On this side,
their frustration glows red at us.

The moon hauls blood
through the world like a long seine.
Like the desired hand at a garden party,
she smooths the long flank of a hill.
Who is where they want to be?

The moon is a wild wind the staunch trees
cannot withstand.
They curl in, defeated, like waves.
They are the moon's slaves.
They shine back at her all night with dumb love.

Eve

Fish swam like commas; a monument
like a grandfather clock spoke of the long time
passing; bones and husks like a picnic's debris
suggested others had left here already:

everything was like something unfamiliar
and corresponded with the infinite
yearning she felt, which could not be appeased
by lemonest yellow or plummest blue.

Some would argue it was a sexual longing
stood up in her at that time with a
not-enough restlessness and sadness,

others, that it was the more humdrum moment
when all ladders point downwards and a snake's hiss
whispers from the grass that we should want more.

Work

The minute hand gone,
the gilded hour hand
circles the blue
face of our public clock
but slowly, as with wings spread, coasting.

Lessons go by like clockwork,
a little rusted. The sere masters
squirrel away. The dry light
swears its fealty to the precise
autumn colours, the dumps of leaves.

A Crane Speaks

Behind the nineteenth-century brick court
you're on the point of entering, I stand
proud and go round as smoothly as a hand
absently leafing through a bland report.
Enter that nineteenth-century brick court:
I go down like the sun. But when the land
is night-blind and the stars are bare, the wind
howls in my bones and, though my rigging's taut,
its whining and my gauntness both recall
mice playing on those weed-cracked concrete beds,
once Mercury's, once Gemini's, when space
was new,
       lost gantries at Canaveral
from which the rockets rose like arrowheads
to smash the heavens' azure carapace.

Boarders

New wind combs the new grass
across the field
that was full of flints
we picked like magpies
or ragpickers
in a forgotten province.

Anywhere is a world.
Those first afternoons
away from home taste
like a freshly-picked blackberry,
brief sweetness bursting
from every cell.

We bent like question-marks
and the wind blew the trees
one way,
their spines
hardened and callused,
the earth all ours.

Prime Numbers

Happy a world
in which the beautiful
is always true.

Get real.
Think, say,
of the tree behind Grandpa Hughes's Bench

oh, thirty years back,
when the old boy
was still alive,
too frail ever again

to make it to the bench
he'd sat on
afternoons enough to become a legend.

I saw him once,
doubled
over his walking-stick.

The bench is gone –
a golf course –
and the tree with it –
and Grandpa Hughes.

I think of prime numbers,
the always-out-there,
prime before they are found

radiant
in darkness

and I think of that tree
black and white in the rain
one wild night,

the always-out-there
gnarled, obdurate,
dripping
and shining.

First Love

In some small town, one indifferent summer
John Ashbery

the summer you wore white – that's what I wrote
in my poem for you, one of the many, the day you
paused, in a short white tennis dress, and had a
word with me, your partner being a friend of mine
I almost hated. It was all in lower case,
I being so bemused, and still

a tossing wooded hillside or a head of black hair
foaming on shoulders or a slant rain
driven in from the west and leadening the landscape
like a teenage mood can revive the longing for you,
sweat pricking palms so that I swear your image
is printed on my heart like Christ's on the veronica,

but would we speak? We rarely did, my adoration
so tongue-tied and beneath you. Once,
in a corridor of our school, I had you read
a different poem. You read it slowly, patiently,
then turned your dark eyes firmly up to mine
and told me, 'You must love her very much.'

Yes, I saw your engagement in *The Times*
twenty-one years back. I imagine for you
dogs, a flagged kitchen, money, children.
This wintry night, sleet tumbling on my skylight,
I remember your brief white tennis dress,
the stir it made in me, and I remember

that your mere being lit the world for ever.

Pips in a Watermelon

I

Can I perceive an object
that isn't here?
                    And is it brought
like a
like a unicorn to a virgin's lap?

The hard nipples of a boy
in a changing-room
twenty-five years ago

as present to me
almost as breath

a moment

II

An afternoon
spent writing/not writing,
listening to the rain
laundering
vacancy for the umpteenth time.

As though a life
were something that would simply come true
if you waited for long enough.

It was like this for years.
There were obsequies and humiliations
and the rain washed and washed
the streaming skylight.

The mind wanders back from abstraction
to a world that is unreal,
too much an instance, too little
the thing itself.

A boat swings at the quay.

III

I leaf not fruit,
leap with the seasons
but not fruit,
jangle my leaves,
an old retainer of the sun.

I have nothing to offer
this wayfarer
who curses me so I shrivel
as though consumed by flame

as though he didn't know I
too get around, I
too am ubiquitous,

for when the first
shepherd passed me
with cagmag flock

out of my dark
multifoliate depths
a voice proclaimed itself

itself.
I was the ground
the Ground of Being needed

to show against,
a darkness
liquid flame played over and through but did not touch.

IV

A boat swings at the quay.

Emma,
your headstone

(with its dates that mark off what seems
a shorter then a shorter time)

has long lost count
of autumns, mowings.

Could I row
to you I would, big with

news like pips in a watermelon.
Your red coat

flashes to mind
like a perpetual flame,

this winter's drifted leaves
another generation

kicked by another
young, thoughtful generation.

V

The world is not a poem
though it was made
nor are the worlds you make
the world, or not yet.

The rain darkens and hardens
and even the joke backwards-turning clock
trudges along with sloped arms,
conscripted, herded minutes
funnelling through a turnstile
like a crowd that slowly drains from the streets
until the streets are empty.

A burger-box rattles and blows about, ajar.

VI

There are two ways to view the islands:
one is on a converted fishing-smack
and the other, for the adventurous, like us,
is to ride on the stiff inflatable
that smacks off the waves like a thing the sea spurns
and wants to mash to pieces. So we went,

out past the Bitches, rocks the grey water drools off,
past the uncounted wrecks I hadn't mentioned,
so terrified we missed the birds we'd come for.
Prayer came, half-remembered, never mastered:
Holy Mary, Mother of God, have mercy on us sinners
now and at the hour of our death

which seemed a shorter, then a shorter, time.

VII

I imagine the unicorn
as on an island
though it might be the depths of any forest
in which it stops

and sniffs, dark liquid eye
dreaming back inwards,
expectant, thoughtful,
intelligent, instinctive.

In boyhood, even then, we should have known
from the foam backed up in a side-stream
you could cross with a step
that we were poisoning the waters.

A galloping consumption
brings earth face to face with itself,
the gaunt, digged ribs,
the technicolor sunsets.

It is darkening rapidly
and the answer has
to be found in whatever
the half-life of a sunset is.

VIII

After a disquisition
there is always a pulling back, a question
there wasn't time or it seemed too pushy to ask
before the speaker was swept off
by the student hosts – the kind of people who trade
on such acquaintance, who laugh knowingly
about how the performance varied last night –
for dinner, or to catch a train home.
It is in that moment of first absence
that the evening escapes into itself
and becomes what it is going to be, something
achieved, delicate, questionable. Just so,

the discovery of any system
of belief is a matter for dismay,
a retreat from the pointillisme
of what is. There is always something over,
a niggle that expands into denial,
isn't that right? But if faith is a way
it's a perpetual beginning, a setting forth
like that of words into the unknown
minutes and years in which they will disclose
their meaning: we wouldn't think of asking
anything if answers could not forthcome, not even
after a disquisition.

IX

Here are the effects
that were left: the desolate
windy tower, the sun's
gorgeous and silent death at sea, the sea
unearthly, glazed. Young
they dazzled me

and I thought to work that estate,
trusty and diligent with nothing
really to live on but my wits.

X

The unicorn may be as randy
as all-get-out, scrotum flexed
as though swept by a stream, a jet of bubbles,
wrinkled with want;
it doesn't matter. His horn

points up to heaven like the Baptist's finger,
ambiguous, androgynous precursor,
to the heavenly country,
gardens watered by running streams.

XI

Times get folded up to each other
like the halves of a sheet in folding,
look into one another, as close
almost as breath.

The smell of grass
blown on a Surrey hillside.

I can almost
smell your skin
and cannot make you smell mine. For a moment,
everything lives again.

XII

Mary, mother
folded about the flame within her,

was not consumed.
Mind comes to matter, soul

to body, lost
time to life

when scrub parts
and the unicorn to the virgin comes.

Everything lives again.

A moment, a boat swings at the quay
liquid flame played over and through but did not touch.

Young, thoughtful generation,
a burger-box rattles and blows about, ajar.

Which seemed a shorter, then a shorter, time,
the half-life of a sunset is,
after a disquisition,
really to live on, but my wits?

Gardens watered by running streams
and the unicorn to the virgin comes.

Everything lives again.
Everything lives again.

Bob Dylan's Minnesota Harmonica Sound

Open-cast mining country, a hole so vast
the diggers looked as tippable as toys
if you stood on the rim and gazed across it;
iron for world wars, iron for Korea,

but thinning. Scraggly grass and mud, the light
grey as age in the early days of autumn,
when first frost prickled and the mountains shook
in the wind that seemed to be always blowing,

blowing and sucking. Shrunken forests,
spruce and fir, pines, moccasin country,
a map freckled with water, bogs absorbing
the blue-green needles of the tamarack.

The freight-train whistles blew and sucked. Their wail
hung in the steady and insistent gusts
like a come-hither fading with the dusk.
Night was indoors, the sound of parents' friends.

All you could be was family or elsewhere.
A boy lounged on the main drag.
He was pretending he was James Dean,
he was pretending he was Baudelaire.

Small wonder, then, if home became a spotlight,
as, blowing and sucking, you count the changes,
wearing a hood like a cowl to shut
out the sound of the everlasting wind

that blows from childhood, blows to suck you back.
There's no solace or ease now for the soul
that kicked the mine-dust from its heels. Sometimes
the one comfort is never standing still.

Not Fade Away

in memoriam Jerry Garcia, 1942–1995

I play one record then another,
hearing your youth
in your later work and your
late economy in your youth's
profligate, glittering runs.

On the Roof of the World

'Hey Jude' was the longest single, up to that time,
ever released. It sweats off, chorus like a mantra.
The times are changing. New musics divide the audience
and skirts are longer, but it's a bright London shopping day
when the traffic stops. Only a black cab moves
gingerly through the crowd, like a toy cruiser nudging weed,
and we're all craning upwards: planks and scaffolding
on the townhouse roof and the clipped, drifting music
the Beatles play. It is their last concert,
though nobody knows this. George twangs his Fender, John
hammers-off on his Epiphone, Paul stomps
with his violin-bodied fretless bass and Ringo, dreamed up
by a manager who died a long time ago, kicks the years
out of his bass drum padded with a rug. How sweet

it would have been, someone will write, to watch them
play the Marquee, this funky little rock'n'roll band.
They are so far above us, we can hardly see them.
They are playing for God. They are playing for cameras
because the show's outgrown the road. We can't believe it.
Tomorrow's papers will acclaim a British institution.
I'll read them and imagine I was there like everyone.
They are already going out of fashion. There's nothing left
but acrimony, separation, lawsuits. The last great single,
'The Ballad of John and Yoko', will be John and Paul
alone, hurrying in midsummer heat, the way it was at the start.
Nobody knows this. They have climbed too far to get back
anywhere we might be among the crowd who clap then drift
    apart
when the helmeted bobbies have the amps turned off.

Ovid: Apollo and Daphne

After the flood, among the bogs and swamps
that were spread out to dry like linen,
the animals appeared, some familiar, some
entirely unknown; it was like the banks
of the Nile when the river wastes away
and the fellaheen who turn up clogs of mud
find a world half-dead, half-alive with crawling
things, offspring of the marriage of warmth and water.
Birds wheeled and cried on wide, fresh-coloured wings.

Whether or not the earth intended it, the first
new creature was the serpent, Pythias, the Python,
who slides into the heart's remotest darkness,
who brought a sick green shadow to the sacred places
he slunk among. Apollo swarmed on him with arrows
whose metal heads were tempered in the sun. That slow
bloody attrition is remembered at the Pythian games
where the young vie for oak-leaf garlands, for all this
took place before Apollo tied green laurel in his hair.

Excitement was still bounding in his veins
when he saw the child Cupid toying with a bow.
'What is this child playing with men's stuff for?'
he ground out. 'It was I who killed the Python.
The carcase rots and stinks along a farm's length.
Run away with your little lamp and go guide lovers!'
But the child rounded on his solar health and smiled.
'True, you can slaughter worlds. It's a human boast,
less than divine, just as your strength is less than mine.'

He stretched and flew off to a toehold on Parnassus,
aimed with his left arm and let slip two arrows.
The first was lead, a sullen, lightless shade:
it shivered when it struck white Daphne's heart and sent her
into her father's arms to vow life-long virginity.
The second, golden arrow pierced Apollo with such
fire that it seemed his bones burned with desire.
One glimpse of Daphne seared along his heart
the way a stray spark will ignite a hayfield.

What he could see – hair curling past her shoulders,
the naked throat, bare arms and eyes to drown in –
thrust him to figure what was hidden by her dress.
The god who speaks to us in caves and temples
of what is past, or passing, or to come,
master of herbs and medicines, god of poetry and music,
was reduced to the passion that cannot be healed
by any wayside sprig or doctor's formula,
or any measured motion of the air. He cried out

'Stay!' but the girl was already running, running faster
the closer he pursued her, ducking and dodging
like a deer, with a deer's wild, liquid eyes; his hands
reached and grasped at the air as it closed behind her.
Wind pressed her dress against her thighs
then ripped it from her, and she ran like a naked hare
as he planned how to circle round and corner her
at the exposed heart of an open field.
She felt his hot breath crawling on her shoulder

as the river flashed into sight. Her father was its god
and she screamed 'Father, save your daughter! Let the green
earth cover her!' She swooned and felt she soared
as skin, taut across muscle, gnarled; fingers and toes

multiplied and divided into branches, roots; her flying hair
thickened into a storm of leaves that slowly settled
as all that had been Daphne changed to laurel.
At the exposed heart of an open field
the tree swayed gently in a gentle wind.

Apollo ran his hands along the boughs and kissed
the slender trunk, hearing her pulse die down with his.
'You who would not consent to be my bride must be the
      badge
of my undying love. For you, generals shall ride in triumph
up to the Capitol with laurel crowns, and where Augustus
creates a city, bronze oak-leaves and leaves of laurel
shall mark out and proclaim a Roman order.'
While he spoke, the leaves of the laurel rustled
as though blessing the new form of his pleasure.

Oxford

Oddbins, which I think opened when we were first married,
   is packed. A pub we met for lunch in, the day
Dylan released *Street-Legal*, has changed name, town not gown,
   so I go to another and sit an hour with
ghosts and a pint. Recalling happiness a thwart thing
   killed hurts me worse than thoughts of the misery
we came to. Sites of memory. The winged years. If this
   is doing work on myself, I don't know, but when
I pass a shop and remember a dress, suddenly,
   after everything, there are tears on my cheek.

Le Cygne

The public gardens, after the divorce,
Pour soulager, ils étaient trop modernes,
les jardins publics, après le divorce
were far too modern to relieve the pain

of the hurt loss you knew was your desert
(quand vos enfants y logeaient chez leur mère),
le mal qui suivait justement votre perte.
when your kids and your ex were renting there.

The earth makes nothing of your bitter gloom.
Mais, aujourd'hui, il faut s'y promener.
La terre oublie toutefois votre amertume:
Today, you walk that melancholy way

and still the swan glides gently like a queen:
encore le cygne glisse doucement comme une reine.

Marfa, Texas

Donald Judd moved there from New York
to make his minimalist sculptures in a place
where they could stay for ever. Cattle country,

sagebrush and cactus, skies with faint Japanese
brushstrokes of tinted cloud; through the roof-to-floor
windows of a junked, remade brick building

the lights are gathered to reflect
on the silvery and expressionless
faces of a hundred waist-high metallic cubes.

The cubes are all the same
except that each has its distinctive feature,
an open top, perhaps, or some plexiglass-shielded

rectilinear internal structure. They say
There is too little space in this world,
leave us alone, they say, *we have nothing to say.*

On hustled days, I think of that place
as of a sudden widening of the street-narrowed sky
to sweep down to the furthest possible horizon.

Acquaintance

The river bank
was a white gash,
chalk spoil
from the new motorway.

I thought of you
in your estranged
apartness orbiting
a nowhere childhood.

We never met
then; seldom, later.
A rackety bar
in Earl's Court.

Sometimes affection
wants nothing bodily
or spiritual,
it's just there,

sudden as rain,
strong as rivers,
stubborn as reeds,
candid as chalk.

A Water-Buffalo in Guangdong Province

at a moment when poems
seem to have stopped

late autumn
it rains in France

where the train surfaces
new building
earthworks revetments
a curving fosse

thin grass
bare poplars
and water standing
in sodden fields

in England seeing
a flooded copse
brought back
a water-buffalo
seen once
wading ponderously

brown water stirring
about its knees

along a paddy-strip
tucked in
between two factories
in southern China

*

heaven is carnal
transfiguring
flesh to a flesh
made incorruptible
that much is known

and to have placed
each foot in turn
flat on the wall
of the lavatory bowl
to get the feel
the girls got
when they danced a dance
with bare feet
at a school in Detroit
or to have brought
earwax and semen
to the tip of the tongue
simply to know

argues a hunger
for world on world

*

mind's restless
quest for what holds
may figure thought
as aiming at a place
beyond change

but sometimes thinking
comes out of living

tentative skeins
smoke lariats
to noose the real

*

I have heard that in Amiens
Apollinaire
conceived a poem
a calligramme
of rain falling
in shaken lines

it rains in France
it rains in Amiens
as hard as any
rain out of Hollywood
bouncing off kiosks
flying like powder
through lights from shops
and café lights

*

time in China
comes very close

hang in the air
like racked clouds
stacked millennia
so that an English
cathedral city
looks gauchely modern

these delicacies
these cubes like cakes
for the sake of example
astonishingly brightly
and sweetly dyed
but savoury-tasting
come from the time your
Henry VIII
was throwing bones
over his shoulder

wide pavements
built to diminish
the passer-by
to bring to mind
how brief his passage
past the forbidding
Forbidden City

*

at close of day
men in white
surgical masks
hose down
the market-place

blood and guts
are swilled away

across the packed
roof-gardens
of Guangzhou
eyes reach
a built horizon

men raised this men
could tear it down

the city's ochre
drinks earth
as a house in childhood
drank light
like the flesh of an apricot

*

people are blaming
people for this
uncanny rain

while a drunk is ejected
rapidly from a café
with a threat of police

apocalyptic
anxieties
are screamed
                or nod
on locked wards
nobody visits

the one policeman
guzzles and farts

                *

to think of rain
hanging like ropes
like the ropes of the nets
of lights that are hung
in late autumn
on trees on the boulevards
of Amiens
        lines
the wind shakes

to wonder whether
that shaking wind
was inspiration

*

the heaven of ideas
could not exist
without the demiurge
to make them real

like the idea
the cobbler has
of the shoe he intends
to make tomorrow

their only purpose
was to be expressed
and once expressed
they entered becoming

were tongues were soles

*

to be a girl
to dance in a dance
with bare feet

to endure derelict
as thin grass
bare poplars
and water standing
in sodden fields

to wade indolently
through brown water
a water-buffalo
in Guangdong Province

For Caroline Fraser

                              Yesterday
I lit a candle for you in the vast
cathedral darkness.
                    Light,
drained of radiance, changes into space.
A tree stretches but can't get out of it.
Each limb points at its vanishing point.
                              Space,
since you died, widened. We are smaller,
more apart in the grey light of 11.30 a.m.

i.m. Clarissa Luard (1948–1999)

Flagstones that guide me workward are simply bare
slabs sounding. Gnawed flint cobblestones I observed
   move when my head moved, yesterday, like
   moonscapes (so, making them move, imagined

I steered my craft, my cockleshell, down to land
like Armstrong, who'd less faith in his instruments
   than in his hands) change back to cobbles,
   molars we crush underfoot and grind flat.

No writer, you served literature out of love.
You could unearth kind words for the shyest stuff,
   so humbling us who wrote but somehow
   making us feel we might touch the moon yet.

Late autumn leaves cling, dithering gently, brown
or golden specks, sparks, glittering in the wind.
   How cold it got, how cold for England,
   when your obituary came this morning.

Poets

1 A Keening

The good poet William Stafford died
a few days back. Oregon grieves
for him, laureate of open space and long grass,
a Kansas boy conscious of limitation.

My neighbour's red globe lightshade makes a whole
room red. Boughs sway between us. Nod. They nod
like knowing that you can't go home again,
hearth-warm and calling though that room is.

I read 'Traveling through the Dark' at school,
his best piece. He decides an unborn fawn
is better dead, and heaves the doe's corpse
off the road and towards the river.

There's a hard knowledge in that poem,
and I wouldn't choose to have had to earn it.
Nobody would. His only swerving
was the compassion that rebukes the world.

2 Thurloe Square, 1995

Ordinary day,
a street of bustling nothing
and a white parked van.

From that top step
Auden's smile was a knowing
benign old lady's smile.

It shifted purple,
pink, white, flecked pyramids of
flesh like rocks shifting.

Tonight, a lamp burns
in the uncurtained window.
I interviewed him.

Twenty-three years on
I'm here by chance, heading for
a poetry do.

Like a boy, he sang
'Chattanooga Choo-Choo', or
believed he sang it

as I believed that
was it. The short *As* of his
half New-York cracked voice,

those holed, odd socks. Rain
lowers my head. Weird dandy
of dishevelment,

grief was the given,
love the elected, burden
of all your poems.

Bubbling, wheezing breath,
like air dragged through two sponges
full of popping soap.

3 San Michele

Cosmopolitan fames. Here is Stravinsky, placed,
with his wife, among graves nobody now brings wreaths,
Russians lost in the first great emigration; here,
overgrowing it, dark laurel obscures the name,
bold, undated, on flat stone, of sad Ezra Pound.

All his madness-aground odyssey at an end,
laurel spreading above, laurel his poems won,
it is just he should lie, here, at the edge of things,
rapt from time like a verse sealed in itself by form.

Sonnet

Suppose there was no great creating Word,
That time is infinite. Corollary?
The present moment gives infinity
An end, by coming after it. Absurd.

Say the beginning of the world occurred
In time, and call that moment moment T;
Everything needed for the world to be
Was, at the point T-minus-x. Absurd.

Falling in love's a paradox like this.
Either it happens like a thunderbolt,
So when it makes our lives make sense, it lies,

Or we had long been hoping for the kiss
That changed us, and, aware how it would jolt
Our beings, we could suffer no surprise.

River Psalm

Swallows are gathering; another autumn
has had enough of us and packs its bags.
We are left to feel desolate or, maybe,
secretly wish that we too could be getting going.
So let us gather at the river
to watch water that seems as clear, as neutral,
as time itself, and to reflect that we wouldn't
even see it if it weren't given shape and sound
by the grain of the land it crosses. If it seems
to sob or chortle – well, perhaps our lives,
tiny as they may be, are added
to a vast chorus that roars in the ears of God.